Christian McCaffrey: The Inspiring Story of One of Football's Star Running Backs

An Unauthorized Biography

By: Clayton Geoffreys

Copyright © 2024 by Calvintir Books, LLC

All rights reserved. Neither this book nor any portion thereof may be reproduced or used in any manner whatsoever without the express written permission. Published in the United States of America.

Disclaimer: The following book is for entertainment and informational purposes only. The information presented is without contract or any type of guarantee assurance. While every caution has been taken to provide accurate and current information, it is solely the reader's responsibility to check all information contained in this article before relying upon it. Neither the author nor publisher can be held accountable for any errors or omissions. Under no circumstances will any legal responsibility or blame be held against the author or publisher for any reparation, damages, or monetary loss due to the information presented, either directly or indirectly. This book is not intended as legal or medical advice. If any such specialized advice is needed, seek a qualified individual for help.

Trademarks are used without permission. Use of the trademark is not authorized by, associated with, or sponsored by the trademark owners. All trademarks and brands used within this book are used with no intent to infringe on the trademark owners and only used for clarifying purposes.

This book is not sponsored by or affiliated with the National Football League, its teams, the players, or anyone involved with them.

Visit my website at www.claytongeoffreys.com

Cover photo by All-Pro Reels is licensed under CC BY-SA 2.0 / modified from original

Table of Contents

Foreword 1

Introduction 3

Chapter 1: Childhood & High School 12

    The Bloodlines 12

    High School 29

Chapter 2: College Career 42

    All Roses 48

    Junior Slump 63

    NFL Draft 67

Chapter 3: Pro Career 71

    Rookie Season 71

    Stardom 76

    Injuries 91

    Back to the Bay 96

Chapter 4: Personal Life 104

Chapter 5: Legacy 108

Final Word/About the Author 110

References 117

Foreword

Since being drafted with the 8th pick in the first round of the 2017 NFL Draft, Christian McCaffrey has accomplished a lot. At the time of this writing, McCaffrey has been selected to two Pro Bowls in 2019 and 2022, and holds a few records, such as the NCAA record for most all-purpose yards in a season (3,864) to go along with being one of three players to ever record 1,000 rushing and 1,000 receiving yards in the same season. It'll be exciting to see what McCaffrey accomplishes in the years to come. Thank you for purchasing *Christian McCaffrey: The Inspiring Story of One of Football's Star Running Backs*. In this unauthorized biography, we will learn Christian McCaffrey's incredible life story and impact on the game of football. Hope you enjoy and if you do, please do not forget to leave a review!

Also, check out my website to join my exclusive list where I let you know about my latest books. To thank you for your purchase, I'll gift you free copies of some of my other books at **claytongeoffreys.com/goodies**.

Or, if you don't like typing, scan the QR code here to go there directly.

Cheers,

Clayton Geoffreys

Visit me at www.claytongeoffreys.com

Introduction

Evolve or die. It's the story for every profession. No matter what you do in this world, you must change with the times. The NFL is no different. The game is vastly different today than it was just 10 years ago.

No position in the NFL has changed more over the history of the league than the running back. The game started with backs as the dominant position—bruising runners who could pound defenders for 30 carries a game were the norm for decades. The likes of Jim Brown, Franco Harris, Gale Sayers, and Larry Csonka ruled the day.

But the NFL came to a realization about 30 years ago: quarterbacks win games, and fans love offense. Since then, the quarterback has become the star, and running backs have become replaceable.

But the running back had to adapt to stay relevant. Fast backs with slick moves soon took over the league. Barry Sanders made the Hall of Fame by making people miss. But the ultimate change was the running back that could run and catch the ball out of the backfield. Teams were now looking for a running back that never had to leave the field. They wanted a running back who could beat a linebacker down the field.

It started in the 1980s with San Francisco's Roger Craig. He became the first back in the league with 1,000 yards rushing and receiving. He was a legitimate force as a receiver. He then handed the baton to Marshall Faulk of the Rams. Faulk and the Rams became the "Greatest Show on Turf," and Faulk, along with Kurt Warner, helped lead the Rams to a Super Bowl win.

Then, for years, running backs went out of style again. But then came Christian McCaffrey. McCaffrey became the first running back since Faulk to have 1,000 yards rushing and receiving, and he was a weapon out of the backfield.

Christian McCaffrey was born into athletic royalty. His maternal grandfather was an Olympic sprinter. His mother was a soccer star at Stanford. His uncle won a national basketball championship at Duke. His aunt was a basketball player at Georgetown. But it was his father who helped pave the way into the league. Christian McCaffrey's father, Ed, was an NFL wide receiver—and a great one. He won two Super Bowls with the Denver Broncos.

When Christian was just two years old, he appeared in *Sports Illustrated*, helping his dad and the Broncos celebrate a Super Bowl win. He was the second of four sons born to Ed and Lisa McCaffrey.

The McCaffreys grew up in the suburbs of Colorado. The family bought a home on a golf course, but the four boys kept ripping up the grass on the course by playing football.

McCaffrey enrolled at Valor Christian High School in the suburbs of Denver with his older brother, Max.

When he entered the school as a sophomore, he was immediately a varsity starter. The team won a state championship and went undefeated during his sophomore year. Max, a receiver, ended up going to Duke to play football.

During his junior and senior seasons, Christian became one of the greatest players in the history of Colorado high school football. He won two more state championships and was named the Colorado Gatorade Player of the Year not just once but twice. He set the state record for all-purpose yards, touchdowns, and career-receiving touchdowns, even though he was a running back.

His mother and father met when they were athletes at Stanford. And like his parents before him, Christian headed to Palo Alto for college. As a freshman, head coach David Shaw limited his playing time and carries. Shaw knew that he had a special player, but he wanted to make sure that McCaffrey understood the offense before he threw him into the fire.

In his sophomore season, McCaffrey had one of the greatest seasons in FBS history. He broke Barry Sanders' record for most all-purpose yards in a season. The Cardinal lost their opening game against Northwestern, but they then won 13 of their next 14 games.

McCaffrey was named the Pac-12 Player of the Year and won the Paul Horning Award. He ended up coming in second place for the Heisman Trophy behind Alabama running back Derrick Henry. It was a controversial decision, with many voters admitting that they did not stay up to see McCaffrey's West Coast games.

After winning the Pac-12 title, Stanford won a trip to the Rose Bowl. McCaffrey went nuts in the game. He set the Rose Bowl record for most all-purpose yards.

After a record-setting season, McCaffrey had to have a letdown. He ended up getting injured and missing a game, but he was not really healthy all season. At the end of the year, he made the decision to leave Stanford after his junior year. He also decided to sit out Stanford's bowl game to train for the NFL draft.

Despite concerns about his size, the Carolina Panthers took McCaffrey with the eighth overall pick. During his rookie season in Carolina, McCaffrey ran into some of the same problems he had during his freshman year at Stanford. There were other running backs taking away carries, so he did most of his damage through the air.

McCaffrey played in his first and only playoff game with the Panthers, a wild card loss to the Saints, at the end of his rookie season.

During his second season in the league, McCaffrey set the Panthers' record for most all-purpose yards in a season. Despite his monster season, the Panthers missed out on the playoffs, and he was not named to the Pro Bowl. He was second team All-Pro.

His third season was one for the ages. He became the second running back in NFL history to have more than 1,000 yards rushing and receiving. He was named to his first Pro Bowl and was first team All-Pro. But despite his spectacular year, the Panthers went 5-11, losing their final eight games. Carolina fired coach Ron Rivera after a December loss to Washington.

After the season, McCaffrey signed a four-year, $64-million contract extension, making him the highest-paid running back in NFL history. But his contract could not save him from injuries. During the 2020 and 2021 seasons, McCaffrey only played in 10 games after suffering a variety of injuries that forced him to miss time.

McCaffrey was back to full health for the 2022 season, but after six games, he was traded to the San Francisco

49ers. Thus, he went from one of the worst teams in the league to one of the best.

He thrived with San Francisco. Ironically, the 49ers head coach was Kyle Shanahan, whose father, Mike Shanahan, was Ed McCaffrey's head coach when he played for the Broncos. Kyle Shanahan was able to use his offensive mind to get the most out of Christian. The 49ers won their final 10 games with McCaffrey. In the playoffs, the 49ers beat the Seahawks and Cowboys, making it all the way to the NFC championship game against the Eagles. Against Philadelphia, the 49ers lost two quarterbacks in the game and only put up seven points in the loss.

Now that he is with the 49ers, Christian McCaffrey is in the perfect situation. He has a great team around him for the first time in his career and an offensive coach who will get the best out of his new running back.

McCaffrey has made himself into one of the great running backs in the NFL, and this is how he got there.

Chapter 1: Childhood & High School

The Bloodlines

If you have ever listened to the Billy Joel song, you know that Allentown is a tough place to call home, especially in the latter half of the twentieth century. Allentown was built up in the post-Civil War boom in the North, as the country moved away from agriculture toward its industrial future.

And Allentown was no different than, say Pittsburgh, Cleveland, or Detroit. The city was booming during the late 1800s and throughout the first half of the 1900s. But after World War II, the population started to migrate from the city into the suburbs. With that, Allentown started to lose a portion of its tax base.

But the real blow to cities like Allentown did not come until the late 1960s and early 1970s. Industrialization started to move into the Northeast and Midwest and head overseas. With that loss of revenue, large factories that once sustained entire towns began shutting their doors.

By the 1980s, Allentown was a city in need of an identity. And like most other former steel towns in Pennsylvania, Allentown turned to sports. It was during this time that Pennsylvania saw a boon in football. This was when the likes of Joe Montana, Dan Marino, Tony Dorsett, and Jim Kelly were lighting up the scoreboard in the Keystone State.

And this was when the McCaffrey family lit up Allentown. Ed, Christian's father, was the first. He was a Parade All-American in football as well as in basketball. He would lead the basketball team to two state championships and leave as its all-time leading scorer. But it was football where he would make his mark.

Ed's sister, Monica, was the girls' basketball program's all-time leading scorer at Allentown Central Catholic High School, where her brother was a star before her.

Monica would end up playing basketball at Georgetown.

The youngest, Billy, may have been the best athlete of the three siblings. He was a freshman when Ed was a senior. It was Billy that came off the bench and helped Allentown Central Catholic win a state championship in basketball. He would go on to break his brother's scoring record at the school.

Billy won an NCAA national championship at Duke, playing alongside Grant Hill, Bobby Hurley, and Christian Laettner. He would later transfer to Vanderbilt and become an All-American. Later in life, he became a Division I men's basketball coach.

"If you mention the name McCaffrey in the Lehigh Valley, everyone knows who you are talking about," Dennis Ramella, the former athletic director at Allentown Central Catholic High School, said. "Even now, the McCaffreys are still the first family of sport in the Lehigh Valley. The whole family was always so unassuming. They had great intellect, were outstanding students and model citizens. They must have been taught those things from a very young age. Those McCaffrey kids were given a gift to be great athletes, but it was their parents who taught them that responsibility came along with the gift."[i]

Ed would end up heading all the way across the country to Stanford to play football for the Cardinal.

Meanwhile, a few miles to the east in Fair Lawn, New Jersey, another family was just starting on its own long line of athletes. David Sime was a three-sport athlete at Fair Lawn High School, playing football, basketball, and baseball. It would be baseball that earned him a scholarship to Duke University.

It was while he was at Duke that David realized he was a great sprinter. In 1956, he was on the cover of *Sports Illustrated*, labeled the "World's Fastest Human." Sime was supposed to compete in the 1955 Olympics but tore his groin while training. He would get his chance in the 1960 Olympics, however, winning a silver medal in the 100-meter race. He nearly won gold in the 4X100, but the team was disqualified for a foul.

While in Rome for the 1960 Olympics, David spent a good amount of time around the boxing team. He befriended a young boxer from Louisville, Kentucky, who would win gold as a middleweight. Eventually, that boxer would change his name and become the heavyweight champion of the world. His name was Muhammad Ali.

After the Olympics, David Sime moved to Miami and became an ophthalmologist. His clients included Richard Nixon, Mickey Mantle, and Ted Williams. He would get married and have three children. His son would become a football player at Duke, and his daughter would be a tennis star at the University of Virginia.

But it would be his daughter Lisa who would become the best athlete in the family. At Ransom Everglades

High School, she lettered in tennis four times and set the school record in the 100-meter. But it was soccer where she excelled.

Lisa scored 56 goals in her career. Like her father, she ended up in *Sports Illustrated*, this time in the "Faces in the Crowd" section. Her skills got her recruited to attend Stanford. At the time, Stanford did not give out scholarships for soccer.

It was in Palo Alto where these two athletically gifted bloodlines collided. How Lisa Sime and Ed McCaffrey met is a bit of a mystery. Each one has their own story, but it's usually the woman who can remember these chance encounters.

"Um, we have a little discrepancy there," Lisa said. "I think we met in preseason in the trainer's room. I was in there getting taped. If he doesn't remember, it's because he was this big-time football player, and I was just this little soccer player."[i]

However, they met, Ed says that it was "love at first sight." Ed would go on to be drafted by the New York Giants. Lisa was a three-year starter at Stanford, but a back injury caused her to miss her senior season.

The couple would marry and have four sons. It was their second son who ended up being the best athlete in either family. Christian McCaffrey was born June 7, 1996, in Colorado. At the time, his father Ed was playing for the Denver Broncos.

Despite Christian's incredible athletic prowess from a young age, Ed and Lisa are careful not to attribute it to the family members that came before them.

"It seemed like they (the media) were trying to find reasons why Christian is good, so they were bringing in other family members, some of whom had nothing to do with his upbringing," Ed said. "No disrespect to any relatives, but they've never even watched Christian play a game in person, and all of a sudden they're a part of the family tree? My brother was a great athlete but didn't even play football. It almost cheapens what Christian's accomplished to try to give credit to other people."[ii]

Family lives can get complicated. We may inherit certain abilities through our genetic bloodlines, but they always come with some baggage, too. For Ed, he moved out west to play college football and did not look back. He never brought his entire family back to Allentown.

For Lisa, things were complicated, too. Her parents divorced, and she remained close to her mother but rarely heard from her father.

"I could write a book on my family," Lisa said. "I had an awful dad. He didn't even know my younger kids' names. He never once came to one of my kids' sporting events. He was abusive, alcoholic, a womanizer, cheated on my mom for 38 years. Hit me several times in the face. Just not a very good person."[ii]

Lisa and Ed channeled the lessons learned from their own childhoods into raising their four boys. Ed describes their parenting technique as "trust and discipline." The boys were allowed to stay home alone from a young age but were not allowed to have cell phones until they were in eighth grade.

When Ed was at Stanford, he took a course called Sleep and Dreams. He has been fixated on the importance of sleep ever since. The boys were never allowed to stay up late, and Ed always discouraged sleepovers, believing that no one actually slept. Phones were always shut off at 10 p.m. so that everyone could get to sleep.

Max was the first of the McCaffrey children. Lisa had a dream that they would have a boy and a girl, and that would be the end of it. When she got pregnant for the second time, Lisa was certain that it was going to be a girl.

"They said it was a boy and for some reason, I just knew in my head that I was going to have all boys from then on," Lisa said. "I just had an inkling, an intuition. So I cried. But I wouldn't have it any other way—I love every single one of them, they're amazing and they all round out the family perfectly and I love them."[iii]

Just because Lisa did not get a girl did not mean that she wouldn't dress Christian up like one. For the first few years of his life, Lisa would dress him up every night like a little girl. She credits that with his sense of style.

While Ed relied on his college courses to help with his parenting technique, Lisa went back to sports to help her with her four boys.

"Sports taught me a lot," she said. "I remember we used to have three-a-day practices during the summer, getting ready for the season. It makes you realize that you can handle it. It makes you realize that you can handle just about anything ... I think it helped me get through childbirth. Seriously. And I know it got me through those 2 a.m. feedings with the kids."[i]

When Christian was two years old, he joined his father, mother, and maternal grandfather on the pages of *Sports Illustrated.* In January of 1998, Ed's Denver Broncos won their first Super Bowl behind legendary quarterback John Elway. After the game, Christian was photographed running through the confetti, and that photo ended up in the magazine. Christian would keep a copy of that photo on his phone for the rest of his life.

Ed and Lisa never pressured the boys to play sports. But given their pedigree, it was only natural for all four of them to make the jump.

"I'll give them direction, but I won't put pressure on them," Ed said when the boys were younger. "I think sports is good for goal setting, and I think it teaches you some important values. So far, Max and Christian seem to love sports. But we'll just have to see. What Lisa and I want is for our kids to grow up to be good people."[i]

Max was the first to enter into the sports arena. He started with soccer, and his mom was his first coach. When Christian saw his older brother on the field, he ran after him and wanted to play too.

In 2001, just after the youngest McCaffrey son, Luke, was born, the family moved to the suburbs about 45 miles south of Denver. They were able to buy a house on a golf course. When the course was empty, the boys would jump into the open green space and start playing. At first, it was soccer, but then it became football.

The boys would set up games on the golf course and quickly started ripping up the grass. The course manager had to have a talk with Ed and Lisa several times, especially when the boys started interfering with the golfers on the course.

The McCaffrey boys were all close in age, and they were always together. Each one had their own distinct personality. Max was the cerebral one, Dylan the introvert, and Luke, the mediator. And then, there was Christian. He was always the happy one.[ii]

Christian is also different in another way—he does not look anything like his brothers. Ed is 6'5" and wiry. Max, Dylan, and Luke all look like their father. Christian, however, is shorter and thicker than anyone else in the family.

"He didn't look like the other brothers, that's for sure," Lisa said. "We joked about it all the time. It was, 'Oh, did the mailman come by? That's weird.'"[iv]

Another thing that made Christian different from his brothers was his competitive nature. No matter what game they were playing, he wanted to win. He also had the ability to replicate any move that he saw on television. When Christian saw a dunk on TV, he would go out to the mini hoop outside and perfectly mimic it.

He also started to use this mimicry skill with football players. He would watch Barry Sanders and later Reggie Bush and copy their moves exactly, replicating what they did on the field. Years later, Christian would play with Barry Sanders' son at Stanford and get to spend time with his childhood hero.

Being the son of an NFL player, Christian spent most of his life around NFL players. While his father was with the Denver Broncos, Mike Shanahan was the head coach. His son, Kyle, ran along the sideline, helping to shag balls during practice and on gamedays, making sure his dad's headset was working properly.

Decades later, the San Francisco 49ers would trade for Christian, and his head coach would be Kyle Shanahan. The story was that Kyle used to babysit the McCaffreys when Christian was younger. This is sort of true, but it was Kyle's sister Krystal who would actually babysit. Kyle usually just tagged along.

Near the end of Ed's career, the Broncos played the Patriots and their young quarterback, Tom Brady. After the game, Christian and his brother went up to Brady for an autograph. He spent some time with the McCaffrey boys, despite the fact that the Patriots had lost the game. Years later, Christian would get his own chance to play against Tom Brady.

When Christian was nine, his parents finally allowed him to play football. In his first game, he scored six touchdowns. It was at that moment that his parents realized there was something different about Christian that his brothers did not have: blazing speed.

When Ed was first drafted by the Giants, he was mocked for his lack of speed. He was not necessarily slow; he just *looked* slow. In college, he was 6'5" and weighed over 230 pounds. He cut weight and started trimming pounds from his equipment to make himself look faster. Ed stopped wearing a belt and even cut the lining out of his pants. Did it make him faster? Not necessarily, but it made him feel faster.

After he was cut by the Giants, Ed caught on with the 49ers and eventually landed in Denver. Even then, he was still mocked by his teammates for being slow. Ed ran the 40-yard dash in 4.69 seconds. It wasn't fast, but it also wasn't slow. However, he was nowhere near as fast as his son Christian.

So, where did Christian get his speed? It was probably his soccer-playing mother. And don't forget her father, Christian's maternal grandfather David Sime, was a famed Olympic sprinter once labeled the "World's Fastest Human.")

In 2000, the Colorado Valkyries were formed in the Women's Professional Football League. Lisa happened to be there as the players were trying out for the team.

A reporter convinced her to run the 40-yard sprint just to see how fast she was. Without having trained much, Lisa ran it in 4.8 seconds, just slightly slower than her husband. But there was a catch.

"I remember being nauseous afterwards, like I had to get food as soon as I finished," Lisa said. "And I remember thinking, something may be going on here because I'm never nauseous like this. And then I realized: Yup, I was knocked up for the fourth time."[iv]

So, after already having three children and being pregnant with her fourth child, Lisa was nearly able to beat her husband in the 40-yard dash.

With his pedigree, every high school in the metro Denver area wanted Christian. But because of their religious beliefs, the McCaffrey family wanted their kids to attend a Catholic high school. Christian made the decision to attend Regis Jesuit High School in Aurora, Colorado.

High School

Colorado high school football is not exactly a hotbed. It is not Florida or Texas, or any of the Southern states for that matter. The best player to ever come out of the state is probably Hall-of-Fame offensive lineman Tony Boselli—that is, until Christian McCaffrey finishes his career.

In Christian's first career game, he took on his older brother Max and Valor Christian High School. One day Valor Christian would grow into one of the best sports programs in the state of Colorado, but at the time, the school was only in its third year of existence.

Max had just transferred to the school the previous season. Like his father, he played wide receiver. Christian played very little in his first game against his brother, but his school, Regis Jesuit, would win the game.

In fact, Regis finished its regular season a perfect 9-0. As the season progressed, Christian got more and more playing time, but his father's shadow was always looming. Ed was a two-time Super Bowl winner and still lived in the area with his family. People in the football world knew him and had strong opinions about him.

In one of his games, Christian was tackled out-of-bounds on the other team's sideline. A coach on the opposing team got into Christian's face while he was still on the ground. The coach started screaming at Christian about his father, including a number of curses.

Instead of getting angry, Christian had the perfect response. He laughed at the coach and told him he was only 14 years old.

Ed did not find the incident funny at all. Instead, he thought about moving the family to another state, perhaps back to Northern California. He was talked down by the boys and Lisa, but they decided that they would start looking for another high school a little further away from Denver. That search would have to wait until after Christian's freshman year was over, however.

In the state playoffs, Regis rolled through the first two rounds. In the quarterfinals, they were able to sneak past Grand Junction by a field goal, and in the semifinals, they survived by a point. In the state finals, Regis ran into a buzzsaw. Mullen High School won all their state playoff games by at least 17 points, and the state championship was no different. They took the title, beating Regis 37-6.

After his freshman year, the family decided that Christian would transfer to Valor Christian to join his brother. Valor had just won the Colorado 4A State Championship, and it was far enough away from Denver that people may have forgotten about the McCaffrey name.

Valor Christian does not really have the look of a high school. It looks more like a college. The school is 35 acres and has a massive library, multiple gyms, and a one-of-a-kind football facility. It costs more than $17,000 a year to attend the school.

The school was in the process of building the best football program in the state of Colorado, and the McCaffrey brothers were going to help that process. Former NFL linebacker Jack Del Rio's son had just enrolled at the school to play quarterback, and now the team had a receiver in Max and a star running back in Christian. With the offspring of former NFL players roaming the halls, it was likely to attract the best talent in the area. Valor now sends two-thirds of its players to play football in college.

By Week 3, Christian was the starting running back at Valor. The McCaffrey brothers helped lead a dominating offensive performance for the school. There was a six-week stretch in which the team scored more than 50 points in each game. The offense ended the season averaging more than 45 points a game.

But it was not just that he was playing for a high-powered offense. McCaffrey had an instinctive skill set that was impossible to teach.

"Physically, there's a good amount of kids that can do it," Valor Christian Coach Brent Vieselmeyer said. "In Christian's case, the mental part was the most impressive. He can process a high amount of information and make changes very quickly. That's hard for a lot of kids (who) have got great athleticism. He's going to start appearing more in different things as he goes through four years. Between playing defense, the things he can do on special teams ... teams won't be able to say, 'We're going to take this kid away, because this is all he does.'"[v]

The Valor Christian Eagles ended the regular season a perfect 10-0. In the state playoffs, they absolutely dominated. In four playoff games, the team gave up a total of 17 points while scoring 218 points, nearly 55 points a game. In the championship game, they blew out Pine Creek 66-10.

Christian never left the field as a sophomore. He played running back on offense, cornerback on defense, and punter and returner on special teams. He had incredible numbers, despite the fact that he spent the second half of most games on the bench, with Valor winning by such a large margin. But even that did not bother him.

"I get to rest my body up, no risk of injury there," Christian said. "I think everyone understands why we come out early."[vi]

Christian had a ridiculous sophomore season for a 15-year-old. He rushed for 1,153 yards and 22 touchdowns. He also added another 657 receiving yards and 10 touchdowns. Max had 833 yards receiving and 8 touchdowns. Just before the season started, Max signed on to play FBS football at Duke.

After Christian's sophomore season, Valor Christian moved from 4A to 5A. The Eagles had won three straight 4A state titles. Now, they would be playing in the largest division in the state.

The Eagles opened the season against 5A Powerhouse Mullen. The game was on ESPN, giving Christian an opportunity to showcase his talents. In the third quarter, the Eagles scored to take the lead but missed the extra point. Late in the fourth, Mullen scored the game-winning touchdown to win the game 14-13. Missed extra points would become a problem for the Eagles.

The following week, Valor Christian traveled to Utah to take on national powerhouse Bingham. The game was a defensive battle throughout. Bingham tied the score with nine minutes remaining.

On their next possession, Christian scored a 13-yard touchdown run to give Valor a 14-7 lead. With less than two minutes remaining, Bingham punted from deep in their own territory. Christian fumbled the punt, and Bingham recovered the ball. They scored to tie the game, sending it to overtime. Then, in overtime, Bingham scored on its possession. Christian scored a touchdown, but Valor opted to go for two and the win. The Eagles failed on the two-point try. They dropped to 0-2.

but after suffering their first-ever 0-2 start, the Eagles started to adjust to the division change and dominate the competition. In the next seven regular season games, Valor Christian scored 352 points, or more than 50 points per game.

In their first four playoff games, the Eagles defense only gave up a total of 30 points. In the state championship, Valor took on Cherokee Trail.

Valor was supposed to win the game big against the underdogs from Cherokee Trail. But Cherokee Trail was able to hold Valor scoreless in the first half for the first time since 2010. The third quarter also ended with both teams tied at zero. On the last play of the third quarter, Christian made a critical play, but as the punter.

Valor was punting, and Christian was able to place the ball on Cherokee's one-yard line. After a three-and-out, Cherokee punted, and a few plays later, Christian scored the game's only touchdown. With less than two minutes remaining, Valor kicked a field goal. The Eagles went on to win the game 9-0.

It was the fourth straight state title for the Eagles. For Christian, he was named the Gatorade Player of the Year for the state of Colorado. He ended the season with 1,390 yards rushing and 23 touchdowns. He also added 665 receiving yards and another 14 touchdowns. For the second straight season, he was named all-state.

With his junior year in the books, Christian could now turn his attention to his college recruitment. Unsurprisingly, he was receiving interest from nearly every Pac-12 and Big 10 school. He had scholarship offers from Notre Dame, Michigan, Oregon, Arizona State, and Ohio State.

Most of the big SEC and ACC schools stayed away, however. There were concerns about his size and speed. But Christian was not just a star on the football field; he was also great on the track. During his junior year, he placed sixth in the 100-meter run and 10th in the 200-meter run in the state of Colorado.

Christian was a four-star recruit and in ESPN's top 300 players in the country. As his junior season came to an end, he made his decision. Like his parents before him, Christian decided that he was going to sign with Stanford University.

If possible, Christian's senior season was even better than his junior year. In the second game of the season, Valor once again traveled to Utah to take on Bingham. Late in the fourth quarter, Christian caught a touchdown pass to tie the game at 21. In overtime, Valor could not score, but Bingham kicked a field goal to win the game. For the second straight season, the Eagles lost in Utah.

Back in Colorado, Valor Christian dominated their opponents. Christian was getting so good that even opposing coaches praised his game.

"He's probably in the top five I've ever seen play," Pomona Coach Jay Madden said. "He's tough and you can't tackle him. He's definitely, in my 20 years of coaching, as good a back as I've seen."[vi]

Valor was so good that, during the month of October, the team went 4-0 and averaged 51 points a game. Christian only carried the ball 17 times in the entire month after sitting out every second half of those four games. The team averaged 51 points a game.

"It makes him a blessing to coach, that's for darn sure," Valor Christian Coach Rod Sherman said. "There was one game in particular. One of our backup running backs is a senior, a really good safety for us, Jace LaMunyon, and we got the ball at the one. We pulled Christian out and Jace scored, and Christian was the first one running on the field to congratulate him."[vi]

The Eagles cruised through the remainder of their schedule and captured their third state title with Christian on the team. In total, the Eagles only lost three games in three seasons, and two of them were to the same team from Utah.

Christian ended his senior season with 1,863 yards and 27 touchdowns. He also had 721 receiving yards and another 16 receiving touchdowns. And realistically, he only played about half of the time for Valor. Christian ended his career as Colorado's all-time leader in touchdowns and points scored, but that did not matter much to him.

"As far as rankings go, I'm only 17 years old," Christian said. "I grew up watching guys like Terrell Davis break records. I couldn't ask for a better O-line, all five of those guys. The film stands for itself. Watch it. They're incredible."[vi]

For the second straight season, Christian was named the Gatorade Player of the Year, and for the third straight season, he was all-state. He also ended his career with 12 varsity letters, having lettered in football, basketball, and track in all four years of high school.

Christian was selected to play in the 2014 U.S. Army All-American Football Game. The backfield was crowded with future NFL talent, including Nick Chubb, Sony Michel, and Joe Mixon. Christian did not get any carries in the game, but he did catch one pass for 15 yards.

And now, it was time to head to his parent's alma mater, Stanford, to show what he could do on the college level.

Chapter 2: College Career

Stanford is not exactly known for producing NFL talent. Sure, John Elway and Andrew Luck came out of Stanford, but can you name another NFL player? Frankly, the school is more known for producing greatness in American life in general. It has produced President Herbert Hoover, writer John Steinbeck, Google Co-Founder Larry Page, PayPal Co-Founder Peter Thiel, and three Supreme Court Justices.

But Stanford *does* have a number of famous athletes who walked its halls, including Tiger Woods, John McEnroe, Katie Ledecky, Kerri Walsh Jennings, and Jessica Mendoza. However, the school does not treat its athletes any differently than normal students.

With so many students who were also famous, everyone just became another student at Stanford. That anonymity allowed Christian to just blend in. For the first time in his life, no one dwelt upon his famous father, they just knew *him*.

Stanford Coach David Shaw intentionally limited McCaffrey's touches at the start of his freshman year. Shaw wanted him to get used to the college game before he started giving him the ball more often. In his first career college game, McCaffrey only had one carry, but he caught a 52-yard touchdown pass and returned three punts for 60 yards. He ended up with more than 100 all-purpose yards, but it was only on five touches.

With the game against FCS school UC-Davis, Shaw even tried to pull McCaffrey from the game, but the kid wanted to stay in his first career game.

"For the record, so everybody knows, I tried to pull him out," said Shaw. "I tried to pull him off of kickoff after that long touchdown reception, because he ran such a long way. He looked at me and smiled and said, 'I'm not coming off.' He goes down on kickoff and makes the next tackle. That's the kind of football player he is."[vii]

After the game, Christian was not satisfied with his effort and wanted to do more for the team.

"There's a lot of things I can work on," McCaffrey said. "I dropped a punt; I've got to fix that. You only get one opportunity to play this game. You might as well play as if it is your last."[vii]

The following week, McCaffrey did not play in a loss to USC. Over the next three games, he would carry the ball four times and have three receptions. The Cardinal went 2-1 in those games, but fans were starting to get restless. They wanted to see the kid play. A 17-14 loss to Notre Dame only upset the fanbase even more, as the offense looked lackluster and had a legitimate shot to beat the Irish.

But Shaw was being cautious with his freshman. He even took McCaffrey off kickoff and punt returns to save his legs, but it was hard to save something that was not being used. At that point, McCaffrey was down the depth chart. And in front of him was the son of his childhood idol, Barry Sanders Jr.

In a win over Washington State, McCaffrey touched the ball five times for 53 yards, but in a loss to Arizona State, he only got two touches for two years.

In a blowout win over Oregon State, McCaffrey started the scoring. On Stanford's opening drive, he caught a 52-yard touchdown. It was his second and last touchdown of the season.

Against No. 25 Utah, McCaffrey saw his most action of the season. He rushed the ball eight times for 77 yards but could not find the end zone. Stanford lost the game in double overtime.

"I'm ready for any situation, whether it's 12 touches a game or two touches a game," McCaffrey said after the game.[viii]

Stanford was now 6-5 heading into "The Game." The Cardinal blew out their rival from across the Bay, and

McCaffrey continued to see the ball more often. He had five touches in the win for 53 yards.

As the season progressed, Stanford's offensive coordinator, Mike Bloomgren, started to realize what he had in McCaffrey. Not only could McCaffrey be dangerous running with the ball but he was also an effective weapon catching it. Bloomgren started designing an offense like the one Chip Kelly ran at Oregon and later implemented with the Philadelphia Eagles.

That offensive would eventually morph into what we know today as the run/pass option, or RPO. But at that time, the offense was more of a read option game, and Christian McCaffrey was perfect for it. Defenses keyed on him, and that allowed the quarterback to pull the ball for big runs.

Slowly, Bloomgren started working more plays into the offense for McCaffrey, but both he and Shaw knew that it would be his sophomore season when it would all come together. The offense was complicated and took time to learn. But Christian spent hours studying. Some nights he would call Bloomgren to help him break down plays on the phone.

Stanford cruised to a win over UCLA and was selected to play in the Foster Farms Bowl against Maryland. The game was played at Levi's Stadium, the home of the San Francisco 49ers, practically Stanford's backyard.

Shaw moved McCaffrey back to punt returner, and that's where he did the most damage. McCaffrey returned four punts for 81 yards, setting up the Cardinal with great field position. He also carried the ball seven times for 51 yards. It was his best output of the season.

Stanford won the game in a blowout. But it was McCaffrey's ability to return punts that grabbed everyone's attention.

"He's had a great season," Stanford senior quarterback Kevin Hogan said. "You might see him in New York in a couple years. That's how good he is."[ix]

Hogan may have been able to see the future because what would come next nearly won Christian McCaffrey the Heisman Trophy.

All Roses

Christian McCaffrey had a relatively quiet freshman season, but that was by design. Coach David Shaw was bringing him along slowly. But both Shaw and offensive coordinator Mike Bloomgren knew they had something special, and it was time to unleash it on the world.

But that would almost immediately hit a speed bump. Stanford traveled to Illinois to take on Northwestern and forgot to bring their game. Every time the Cardinal started to get something going, a penalty ended the drive or a turnover gave the ball back to the Wildcats.

Every time something went right, Stanford shot themselves in the foot.

The Cardinal lost the game 16-6. It was the first time in nine years that they did not score a touchdown, and it snapped a 95-game streak of scoring at least 10 points.

Despite the loss, there were flashes of what McCaffrey would soon be throughout the season. He ran the ball 12 times, caught 5 passes, and returned 4 kickoffs. The offense just wasn't there yet.

The Cardinal recovered the following week against Central Florida. McCaffrey touched the ball 27 times for 166 all-purpose yards and a touchdown. He also had an 80-yard punt return for a touchdown called back on a controversial block-in-the-back call.

"We're going to stretch him thin," Shaw said. "He's going to get more comfortable each week. We're just scratching the surface for what he can do."[x]

While it was nice to get a win over UCF, Stanford's next opponent would be their first real test. The Cardinal headed south to Los Angeles to take on sixth-ranked USC. It was a back-and-forth game, but Stanford put up 10 points in the fourth quarter to win 41-31, proving that they were Pac-12 contenders.

McCaffrey had another stellar performance. He rushed for 115 yards on 26 carries. It was his first career 100-yard rushing game. He ended the game with 249 all-purpose yards. But more importantly, it was a huge win for the Cardinal.

"The guys were celebrating after the game, but I reminded them we don't get a trophy for this one," Shaw said. "It's a regular season game against a conference opponent that we won on the road. That's great. But we get back to work. We get one night to celebrate and we need to get ready to play next week."[xi]

The more McCaffrey racked up yardage on the field, the more Shaw and the offensive staff trusted him.

"He is a manifestation of everything you preach as a coach," Shaw said. "It makes it easy for me. I just say, 'Do it like him.'"[ii]

His teammates started to recognize his importance and his leadership. Before every game, the Stanford football team votes for one player to carry out the flag before the team runs on the field. It is usually a senior. McCaffrey was voted by his teammates to carry the flag. He was the first underclassman ever chosen for the honor.

The following week, McCaffrey had the best game of his career up to that point. The Cardinal moved to 21 in the FCS rankings and did not suffer a letdown against Oregon State.

McCaffrey rushed for 206 yards for the first time in his career and had 303 all-purpose yards, the first time he broke 300 yards in his career. It was an epic game, and a huge win over the Beavers.

"What else can you say about Christian McCaffrey," said Shaw after the Oregon State win. "He's physical, he's tough running between the tackles. He's fast and explosive and ready to make the big plays."[xii]

The following week, McCaffrey scored his first rushing touchdown of the season against Arizona. Through five games, he rushed for 601 yards but only scored one rushing touchdown. When the Cardinal got close to the goal line, they would put a bigger back into the game to take it over the line.

McCaffrey should have been called the mayor because, in 2015, he just ran Los Angeles. Against USC, he had a great performance, but against UCLA, he had a *legendary* performance.

He ran for 206 yards and 4 touchdowns. He also returned two kickoffs for 122 yards in a blowout win.

"That Northwestern loss did something to us, it bonded us together," McCaffrey said. "A lot of teams fold after a loss like that first game and a lot of people were against us and we remember that. It continued to push us and it will continue to push us because you can't forget where you come from. That's definitely a lot of fun to go out there and see holes and make plays. It makes people scream a lot, but there still are no trophies at the end of that. We got a lot of football left. We got a lot left in the tank and we got to move on and look to next week."[xiii]

Since the opening loss to Northwestern, Stanford won five-straight games by more than 10 points. They were quickly moving up the FBS polls. And Christian McCaffrey was starting to get serious buzz for the Heisman Trophy. But for him, he just wanted to keep winning games and beating down his opponents.

"We need to keep playing pissed off," McCaffrey said. "People think that we're just a bunch of nerds. I just want to become a new being when I walk onto the field. It's about finding that animal inside of you, finding that beast that can go 60 minutes of fast, physical football."ⁱⁱ

McCaffrey clearly was not done. The following week against Washington, he once again had more than 300 all-purpose yards against the Huskies, practically leaving his coach speechless.

"I'm at the point where I don't know what else to say, other than watch him," said Shaw. "The little guy never gets tired. He's just special."ˣⁱᵛ

Through seven games, McCaffrey was leading the nation in all-purpose yards, averaging 253 per game. For the first time all season, he had more than 100 yards rushing and receiving, and he scored a touchdown doing both.

Against Washington State, Stanford got a little lucky. McCaffrey carried the ball 30 yards to set up the go-ahead field goal with less than two minutes remaining, but the Cougars drove the ball down the field and missed a game-winning field goal as time expired. It kept Stanford's seven-game winning streak alive.

And just when everyone thought they had seen everything that Christian McCaffrey could do, he pulled something else out of his bag of tricks. In his first game in his home state, he threw a touchdown pass against the Colorado Buffaloes. Early in the fourth quarter, McCaffrey took a pitch and threw a perfect 28-yard touchdown pass to seal the victory for the Cardinal. He also rushed for more than 100 yards for the seventh-straight game, tying a school record.

"We've been working on it for a while," said Shaw of McCaffrey's touchdown pass. "Needless to say, he was a little excited."[xv]

Stanford was now number seven in the country and had a realistic shot at a national championship if they could just win out. But up next was a tricky Oregon team. As time wound down, Stanford scored a touchdown that put them down by two. They went for the conversion but failed. They lost the game by two.

In the game, McCaffrey set two school records. He was now the school's all-time leader in all-purpose yards in a season and had the most consecutive games with 100 yards rushing. But it was little condolence after such a tough loss.

But the Cardinal bounced back with a nice win over Cal in "The Game." In their final regular season game, Stanford hosted Notre Dame. With 30 seconds remaining, the Irish scored a touchdown to take a one-point lead. McCaffrey had a nice return on the ensuing kickoff, and the Cardinal were able to move the ball into Irish territory. As time expired, Stanford kicked a game-winning 45-yard field to beat Notre Dame.

The Irish were the first team to hold McCaffrey under 100 yards since Week 2, breaking his school-record streak.

Stanford won the PAC 12 North Division and earned a spot in the PAC 12 Title Game against USC. McCaffrey saved his best game for last. In the blowout win, he amassed 461 all-purpose yards. He rushed for 207 yards and a touchdown, and he had 105 receiving yards and a touchdown. He even threw another touchdown pass. It was an unreal effort.

"He's the best football player in the nation," said Shaw. "I don't know if there's any question. Nobody in the nation is doing what he is doing. It's not even a debate."[xvi]

In the game, McCaffrey broke Heisman Trophy winner Barry Sanders' record for most all-purpose yards in a season. Sanders was his idol growing up, and McCaffrey even got to play with his son and spend time with the elder Sanders.

"It's a huge honor," said McCaffrey, who had a poster of Sanders on his bedroom wall as a boy. "I couldn't do it without my teammates. I can't tell you how much I love those guys. It takes all 11 guys on the field doing their job to make that happen. I love this team."[xvi]

As the winner of the PAC 12, Stanford earned a trip to the Rose Bowl. But first, McCaffrey had to make a stop in New York. He was one of three players invited to the Heisman Trophy ceremony in New York City. Besides McCaffrey, Alabama running back Derrick Henry and Clemson quarterback Deshaun Watson were also invited.

But McCaffrey was at a disadvantage. He was up against two of the best players from powerhouse eastern universities, while he attended Stanford.

"People treat you just like they would treat anybody else—there's positives and negatives to that—but Stanford is just a different place," McCaffrey said. "You realize that half of the school is not from the United States and they've never watched American football. These are the same people who are future owners of Fortune 500 companies. And so, for me, I had to take advantage of meeting them, and getting to know them, and seeing what they're doing. I think it humbles you. It reminds you who you are, and it makes you realize that life is a lot bigger than football sometimes."[xvii]

There was also another problem with McCaffrey's candidacy. Half the country had never seen him play. The average start time of his games was 10:30 p.m. EST, meaning that the majority of the east coast was in bed by the time he took the field. Either way, he was up against some stiff odds.

The award ended up going to Henry from Alabama by 88 votes. McCaffrey came in second place, but most of the country still believed that he should have won it, even if it didn't bother him.

"You just have to laugh it off," McCaffrey said. "At that point, I knew that I didn't win any of the awards in Atlanta. So, I figured I wasn't going to win the Heisman. When you're young, and you have these big aspirations, and you want to win them, it's great. But I've actually learned a lot since then. I've learned that you really can't focus on what is out of your control. Winning games is a lot more fun than receiving awards."[xvii]

While McCaffrey broke Barry Sanders' record for most all-purpose yards in a season, Henry broke Herschel Walker's SEC record for most rushing yards in a season. But Henry played at Alabama, and McCaffrey at Stanford, and that played into it for some voters.

"Let's face it, to me the Heisman Trophy has become the best player who is on the best team who makes the biggest plays on the biggest stages throughout the season," ESPN College football analyst Chris Low said. "Remember, Christian went off in the Rose Bowl. Well, the award already had been voted on by then. People forget that. I voted for Henry, but McCaffrey was a guy you knew was a great player. It's like every other race; if people want to say he was robbed, talk to the Tennessee people when Peyton Manning didn't win it in 1997."[xviii]

But there was also another issue about why McCaffrey may have missed out on some votes. It was because he was a white kid from an upper-class background, and people felt that he could not be a great running back coming from such a place. McCaffrey's father, Ed, took exception to that portrayal.

"There are immediate stereotypes about a white running back who grew up in the suburbs of Colorado," Ed McCaffrey said. "When we've gone to camps or all-star games, he walks on the field and people look at him like he's nothing."[xix]

McCaffrey tried to brush off the criticism, but it was not easy for him to move on.

"When you read about white athletes these days and white skill position receivers specifically, one word you'll always find is tough. You'll rarely see explosive, athletic, stuff like that," McCaffrey said. "You get a little bit upset. People do the eye test and underestimate me, so I do play with a chip on my shoulder."[xx]

That chip helped McCaffrey dominate the Rose Bowl game against Iowa. Eleven seconds into the game, he caught a 75-yard touchdown pass, and he returned a punt for a touchdown to start the second quarter. By halftime, Stanford was up 35-0.

Coming into the game, Iowa was 12-1, with its only loss coming in the Big 10 title game. But Stanford took them apart. McCaffrey ended the game with 172 yards rushing, 105 yards receiving, and 2 touchdowns. He was named the game's MVP.

McCaffrey ended his sophomore season with 2,019 rushing yards, 28th most in FBS history. He set the FBS record with 4,035 all-purpose yards and scored 15 touchdowns. He also threw for two touchdowns.

Junior Slump

With a season for the ages, there was only one-way Christian McCaffrey could go after his sophomore season: down. It was inevitable. But for the first three weeks of the season, it appeared as though everything was going to be just fine.

Stanford rolled to easy wins over Kansas State, USC, and UCLA, and McCaffrey rushed for more than 100 yards in each one of the games. Then came Washington. The Cardinal traveled north to take on the Huskies. Both teams were ranked in the top 10 at the time, but only one showed up for the game. The Huskies demolished the Cardinal 44-6.

"We got ourselves behind the eight ball, by not being able to stop them, and then not being able to convert our third downs, and staying in manageable third downs," Shaw said. "That's just a bad recipe, in particular on the road."[xx]

The following week against Washington State, Stanford was again getting blown out when, midway through the third quarter, McCaffrey left the game and did not return.

"McCaffrey did get banged up," Shaw said. "But there was no reason to put him in late in the game. We just left him out. We'll see how he is during the course of the week."[xxi]

McCaffrey suffered a hip injury. It was bad enough that he had to sit out the following week against Notre Dame. Stanford was able to get a win without him. He returned to the lineup the following week against Colorado, but the Stanford offense turned the ball over four times and lost 10-5.

With half their season over, Stanford was now 4-3. McCaffrey's streak of more than 200 all-purpose yards was broken. He now had two games in a row without more than 200 yards. It appeared Stanford's PAC 12 hopes were gone, and McCaffrey's run at the Heisman was over.

But just then, McCaffrey went on a tear. Against Arizona, he rushed for 169 yards and 2 touchdowns. He added another touchdown receiving. Against Oregon State, he rushed for 199 yards and a touchdown. And against Oregon, he rushed for 135 yards and 3 touchdowns.

But McCaffrey saved his best effort for Cal in "The Game." McCaffrey rushed for 284 yards and 3 touchdowns, all in the second half of the victory. It was the most rushing yards in a game in school history.

"We knew we wanted to run the ball," said Shaw, whose team gained 357 on the ground and 555 overall. "When the game got to the nitty-gritty we wanted to give it to No. 5."[xxii]

The Cardinal ended the season with a win over Rice. McCaffrey again rushed for more than 200 yards and added 2 touchdowns. What Stanford fans did not know was that would be the last time they would see McCaffrey in uniform for the Cardinal.

Stanford was invited to play North Carolina in the Sun Bowl in Tempe, Arizona. Behind the scenes, McCaffrey had already decided that he would leave Stanford and head into the NFL draft. But two weeks before the game, he made his final decision.

"Very tough decision, but I have decided not to play in the Sun Bowl so I can begin my draft prep immediately," McCaffrey wrote on Twitter. "Thx to all my teammates for their 100% support—It means a lot to me. Go Cardinal!"[xxiii]

And just like that, his career at Stanford was over. In his sophomore and junior seasons, McCaffrey rushed for 3,622 yards and 21 touchdowns. He added 955 yards receiving and 10 touchdowns. And now he was off to the NFL, like his father before him.

NFL Draft

Despite all his college success, there were still some questions about Christian McCaffrey heading into the 2017 NFL Draft. But at the combine, he put some of those doubts to rest. He ran a 4.48 40-yard dash. He also enticed teams with the various positions he could play and his ability on special teams.

"Something I really pride myself on is not just being a running back that can catch the ball, but if I move out to the slot, I become a receiver," McCaffrey said. "If I move out to 'X' or 'Z,' I become a receiver and not just a running back. I really try to pride myself on route running, catching and being able to be a mismatch anywhere on the field."[xxiv]

The other question that people wanted to know was how dedicated McCaffrey was to football after skipping his team's bowl game. But luckily, he had two of his dad's famous friends who were able to stick up for him. John Elway was Ed McCaffrey's quarterback while he was in Denver. Elway was also a Stanford alumnus who worked to get himself traded to the Broncos on draft day. Elway was also the Broncos' general manager.

"You know what, I understand it now," Elway, who met with McCaffrey before the draft, said. "Obviously when I thought about it, kind of the old school in me wanted to come out and say, 'Why? Why would those guys not play? It's their last game,' and this and that. But I tell you what, when you look at where the league is now and you talk about the value of these contracts for these players coming out and the risks that they're taking, the old salty guy in me got flipped back to understanding. I understand why they didn't play."[xxv]

John Lynch was San Francisco's general manager and played with Ed McCaffrey at Stanford. He also came to the younger McCaffrey's defense.

"As a Stanford fan, I wasn't a huge fan of that," Lynch said. "I think you understand their perspective, but I don't necessarily think it's a positive thing for college football. This is such a team sport—I know there are people that I've talked to here that that really bothers. I'm fortunate. With one of those players, I happen to know the young man (McCaffrey). So, I would never question his commitment to team, but other people will."[xxv]

But McCaffrey had the best answer to any questions that were asked about him skipping the bowl game.

"I just tell them how it is," he said. "When they ask, I'm extremely honest with them, and then we move on to now and playing football," McCaffrey said. "I just know I made that decision, it's a career decision, it was a man decision, to try to protect my dream of playing and succeeding in the NFL. And whether it gave me an advantage or not, I stuck with it and I'm here now moving on."[xxv]

With questions answered, McCaffrey was still expected to go in the middle of the first round. As the draft progressed, Stanford's teammate Solomon Thomas was the third pick by the 49ers. The first running back off the board was Leonard Fournette out of LSU, who was drafted by Jacksonville with the fourth pick.

And then, with the eighth pick, the Carolina Panthers selected Christian McCaffrey out of Stanford. He was now on his way to play with former-NFL MVP Cam Newton and the Panthers.

Chapter 3: Pro Career

Rookie Season

It is never easy being a rookie in the NFL. You have to adjust to the strength and the speed of NFL players. But Christian McCaffrey was no ordinary NFL rookie. He was practically born on an NFL field. When he was two years old, he was in *Sports Illustrated* in a photo during the Super Bowl. So, he knew what to expect from the league.

An NFL rule did not allow rookies to participate in off-season activities until their college finished exams. Stanford did not finish until the end of May, so McCaffrey missed most of the team's activities in the spring. But when he arrived at camp, he started to turn heads with his athleticism and ability to catch the ball out of the backfield.

"I can tell you now there's not going to be anybody in this league that can cover him one-on-one," fellow running back Jonathan Stewart said. "He's a special player."[xxvi]

McCaffrey spent most of camp making Panthers' defenders miss him.

"I had to find different ways to make my older brother miss," McCaffrey said. "A lot of that quickness and setting people up and being able to jab one way and go the other way and explode off that first step—that's where I did a lot of that stuff."[xxvi]

Stewart was going to be the back with the most carries for the Panthers. McCaffrey was going to be used as a receiver out of the backfield, and he would get a handful of carries every game as a change of pace. The Panthers were coming off a disappointing 6-10 season after having played in the Super Bowl the year before.

In Week 1, McCaffrey headed back to the Bay Area to take on the 49ers. He had his first career fumble but also had 92 all-purpose yards. It was not the 200-plus that he was used to in college but it was a good start, and the Panthers won the game.

Every week, Christian would get a handful of carries but did most of his damage as a receiver out of the backfield. In a Week 3 loss to the Saints, he had his first career 100-yard receiving game. It was not until a Week 5 win against Detroit that McCaffrey caught his first career touchdown pass.

After seven weeks, the Panthers were 4-3. McCaffrey was on pace to break Reggie Bush's rookie record for most receptions by a running back, but he still only had one touchdown.

Over the next eight weeks, Carolina went 7-1. McCaffrey scored his first career rushing touchdown and continued to catch touchdowns. In Week 10, he had his first two-touchdown game against the Miami Dolphins. Now at 11-4, the Panthers were tied for the NFC South title with the Saints. The winner would get a home game, and the loser was on the road for a wild card game.

The Panthers traveled to Atlanta for the last game of the season. If the Falcons won, they would have a chance to make the playoffs too. The teams played a tight first half, 7-7. In the second half, Atlanta kicked five field goals, and Carolina could only manage a single field goal. Cam Newton threw three interceptions, and the Panthers lost the game.

Carolina now had to travel to New Orleans to take on the Saints. In two meetings in the regular season, New Orleans beat Carolina twice by a combined 31 points.

Drew Brees carved up the Panthers' defense. Heading into the fourth quarter, Carolina was down 24-12. After a Greg Olsen touchdown catch, the Panthers cut the lead to five, but rookie running back Alvin Kamara scored a touchdown to put the Saints back up by 12.

With five minutes to go, the Panthers got the ball back deep in their own territory. Newton hit McCaffrey on a short pass and he was off to the races. He scooted down the sideline for a 56-yard touchdown reception—his first career playoff touchdown.

The Panthers had the ball deep in New Orleans territory with less than a minute remaining. The Saints' defense pressured Newton into an intentional grounding penalty. On fourth down, Newton was sacked on the New Orleans 35-yard line to end the game. The Saints won 31-26. It would be the first and only playoff game that McCaffrey would ever play with the Panthers.

McCaffrey had a solid rookie season. He had 435 yards rushing and 2 touchdowns. He also added 80 receptions for 651 yards and 5 touchdowns. His 80 receptions were the fourth most in NFL history of a rookie running back. Kamara, who had just beaten McCaffrey's Panthers, had the third most in NFL history with 81. New York Giants running back Saquon Barkley would break both of their records.

It was a good start, but as usual, McCaffrey was his harshest critic.

"I think I fell short in a lot of areas," McCaffrey said. "But at the end of the day, you have to let the game come to you and learn from it. It was a lot of hard work, looking back. It was exciting. And now I know the things I need to improve on for next year. I'm going to get to work on fixing those. It's been an incredible learning experience, for sure. A lot of good, a lot of bad, and overall I'd say it was a good year. I'm trying to become a complete back. I want to be a guy who doesn't have to leave the field. I'll be working my butt off this offseason to get better."[xxvii]

And that's exactly what happened.

Stardom

In the offseason, Jonathan Stewart left the Panthers. The load was now squarely on Christian McCaffrey's shoulders. The Panthers were looking to build on their

11-5 season and got off to a great start to the 2018 season.

After a Week 1 win over Dallas, McCaffrey tied the Carolina Panthers record with 14 receptions in a Week 2 loss to Atlanta. He followed that up with a career-high 184 rushing yards in a Week 3 win over Cincinnati.

"He's a total running back," Cam Newton said. "This is not a fluke. He has been doing this his entire career, collegiately and professionally. The fact that we have a special talent, you can't really gear in using packages for him."[xxviii]

Now that Christian McCaffrey was Carolina's featured back, he was starting to get the hang of the NFL. He began to feel comfortable and it was starting to show in his play.

"The more and more I go through this league I learn that it's never been about proving anyone wrong or proving anybody right," McCaffrey said. "It's proving myself right, and that's the biggest thing that I've had to mentally take over as I continue to grow."[xxviii]

In a Week 4 win over the Giants, McCaffrey scored his first touchdown of the season. But despite having great numbers, he still was not seeing the end zone as much as he would have liked. Just like in college, when the team got near the goal line, he would get pulled out of the game for a bigger back. And with Cam Newton at quarterback, sometimes Carolina did not even need a running back.

Through eight games, the Panthers were cruising. The team was 6-2 and in first place in the NFC South. Everything was looking great for Carolina. But then they headed to Pittsburgh.

McCaffrey had one of his best games as a professional. He caught two touchdown passes and ran for another one. He rushed for 77 yards and caught 61 yards. In any other game, an output like that from him would have meant an easy win for the Panthers—but not on this day.

Steelers quarterback Ben Roethlisberger threw five touchdowns, and worse still, Newton kept throwing passes to the other team. The Panthers were blown out 52-21.

Some pundits speculate that this game could have easily been chalked up to the Panthers having to travel for a Thursday night game. Since the NFL started its Thursday night games, they have been sloppy. It is extremely difficult for a player to recover from playing a game on Sunday by Thursday, especially when you are the traveling team. As such, not only does that team often not play at their best but players also frequently get hurt during these games.

But that loss to the Steelers revealed larger issues within the team. The truth was that Cam Newton always had a problem with interceptions, but now he was running for his life. The Panthers offensive line had allowed five sacks against the Steelers, and Newton was hit a dozen more times.

The game also revealed holes in the Panthers' defense. Not only did Roethlisberger have a huge game, but Pittsburgh could seemingly run whenever it wanted.

The Pittsburgh loss would be the start of a seven-game losing streak for the Panthers. Carolina would lose the next five games by a combined 20 points. In a Week 12 loss to the Seahawks, McCaffrey had 125 yards rushing, 112 yards receiving, and 2 touchdowns. But the Panthers still fell by three points.

In Week 16, the Panthers lost to the Falcons and were eliminated from the playoffs. In the final game of the season, McCaffrey barely played as the Panthers ended their losing streak with a win over the Saints. New Orleans was 13-2 heading into the game, and they had already clinched the top seed in the NFC. The Saints did not play any of their starters in the game.

Carolina finished the season at a disappointing 7-9. But nevertheless, Christian McCaffrey had a breakthrough season. He rushed for 1,098 yards and 7 touchdowns. He added 867 yards receiving and another 6 touchdowns. He was third in the NFL in all-purpose yards behind Saquon Barkley and Ezekiel Elliott. He was named the Carolina Panther team MVP. He was also second team All-Pro.

But for some reason, McCaffrey was not named to the Pro Bowl. It was a snub that no one really understood.

"It is what it is, man," said McCaffrey. "It's been my whole life; nothing new. There's a Drake line that I can always refer back to. He says, 'I don't have to prove anything to nobody except myself.' That's what I've taken, a quote I keep leaning back on. I think it's true. Nobody has higher goals for me than me. I keep those to myself obviously, but I'll continue to use that as a chip, continue to use it as fuel to my fire."[xxix]

In the offseason, McCaffrey headed home to Colorado. He sought out his high school track and field coach, Brian Kula. Kula had left Valor Christian High School and was now running a sports performance school. McCaffrey was looking to get faster and needed Kula's help.

"I look at a running back as a sprinter. And running is actually in the title of my job, my occupation. My job is to run, and it's to do it fast," McCaffrey said. "Everything I do is really pertinent to track. All of my speed work is with a track coach. All of my lifting is with a track coach. Those are the fastest people in the world. And at my position, being fast does not hurt. It's a very big track-based program."[xxx]

Kula created a program for McCaffrey that involved both weight and track training. It helped him to increase his speed, but also keep his muscle.

"I always tell him we don't just do things to burn calories," Kula said. "The intensity we work at is very high, but our volume is quite low probably compared to a Division I college football program. There's several reasons for that. One of them is science—the system we're trying to develop falls within (a certain) sets/reps and volume. When you're after that system, the type 2b muscle fibers, then you're going to require a lot of recovery or you're just going to have overuse and you're not going to get full benefit … It takes five minutes for your ATP system to fully replenish. We're going to make sure that even though it makes the session quite a bit longer, we get proper recovery and (then) full output when we go to do the movement."[xxx]

But the key to these workouts was rest. Christian had to make sure that he was giving his body time to recover from these intense workouts. Just like his father believed in the power of sleep, Kula wanted McCaffrey to take time in between sets to recover before moving on to the next set. The results were immediate.

"I feel the best I've felt in my whole life in terms of being in good physical condition, speed, strength, all that," McCaffrey said. "Why I train (this) way is because I've tried everything. I feel like when I do (this), that's when I feel the best. That's when I can feel growth, I can feel myself getting faster, I can feel myself getting stronger."[xxx]

When he arrived at training camp for the start of the 2019 season, both teammates and fans were amazed by the transformation in McCaffrey. He had lost body fat and gained muscle without gaining any weight. He looked sculpted.

In Week 1, the Panthers took on the defending NFC Champions, the Los Angeles Rams. McCaffrey went off on the Rams. He rushed for 128 yards and 2 touchdowns and added 81 receiving yards. But two costly Newton turnovers hurt the Panthers. Newton threw an interception with less than six minutes remaining in the game that led to a Rams field goal. That sealed the win for LA.

In Week 2 against Tampa Bay, Carolina suffered a devastating loss. Late in the game, the Panthers were down by six with the ball at Tampa's two-yard line. On a fourth-and-one, McCaffrey was forced out of bounds behind the line of scrimmage. Tampa got the ball back and ran out the clock to seal the win. But losing the game was not the worst part. After the game, Cam Newton was diagnosed with a Lisfranc injury to his left foot. (And the truth was, the injury had been plaguing him since the preseason and hampering his mobility in every game.) He went on injured reserve and would not return for the rest of the season.

With their quarterback on the bench, the Panthers would now have to rely heavily on McCaffrey to win games—and he answered the call. The Panthers even went on a four-game winning streak without Newton. McCaffrey scored five rushing touchdowns and two receiving touchdowns in those four games. He added 453 yards rushing.

The Panthers were now cruising along without Newton. They had backup QB Kyle Allen filling in at the helm, and trusted in McCaffrey to win them games. On October 6th, the Panthers beat Jacksonville. Ron Rivera became the team's all-time winningest coach, passing John Fox.

Week 7 saw the Panthers blown out by the 49ers, but they rebounded nicely with a win over the Titans. McCaffrey had three touchdowns in the win over Tennessee; they were the only three touchdowns the Panthers scored in the game.

After eight weeks, Carolina was 5-3, and they were sitting in position to play in the wild card game. Without Newton, McCaffrey was carrying the team. He was on pace to become the third running back in NFL history with 1,000 yards receiving and rushing.

But then injuries began to take their toll with the Panthers. They had already lost Newton, and over the course of the next eight weeks, the Panthers would put three tackles and two guards on injured reserve for the season. Losing their quarterback was one thing, but losing nearly their entire offensive line was another.

It started with a loss to the Packers, and then another one to Atlanta. And the losses just kept coming. After a Week 13 loss to Washington, the Panthers fired head coach Ron Rivera. Earlier in the year, he had become the team's all-time winningest coach. Now, he was out of a job.

"I believe this is the best decision for the long-term success of our team," Panthers owner David Tepper said in a statement. "I have a great deal of respect for Ron and the contributions he has made to this franchise and to this community. I wish him the best. I will immediately begin the search for the next head coach of the Carolina Panthers."[xxxi]

Rivera was hired by the Panthers before the 2011 season. He led the team to four NFC South Division titles and to the Super Bowl. Secondary coach Perry Fewell took over coaching duties for the final four games.

However, it did not seem to matter who the coach was for the Panthers. The losses just kept piling up. Heading into the final game of the season, there was very little drama for the Panthers. The team was not going to make the playoffs, but McCaffrey only needed 67 receiving yards to reach 1,000.

"This man is writing himself into the history book," Carolina safety Tre Boston said. "He's showing us what we will have next year and I think that is important. This is going to be a big offseason for us and you are going to want guys to come here and play. And when you have guys like Christian, who wouldn't want to be his teammate? Who wouldn't want to be on an offense with that guy?"[xxxii]

The Saints demolished the Panthers in the final game, but McCaffrey scored a touchdown and had 72 yards receiving to get himself over 1,000 yards for the season.

"Every year I write down little goals and that was one of them," said McCaffrey. "It's cool when you accomplish one of the goals you write down, but obviously, I can't reiterate this enough, but the most important statistic is winning."[xxxiii]

While Christian McCaffrey had a season for the ages, the Panthers had one in the books that they would rather forget. They ended the year at a dismal 5-11, losing their final eight games.

"The most important stat is winning and we didn't get that done this year," McCaffrey said. "The individual statistics, they're great and cool and stuff you can look back on and be proud of yourself, but we would love to get this thing fixed and fixed quick. It takes a village and football is not easy. It's not a one-man show and it never has been. You look at some of the best teams in the world and they play great team football."[xxxiii]

The fact was, McCaffrey really was a one-man show that season, accounting for a whopping 43% of the team's offensive yards. He ended the season with 1,387 yards rushing and 15 touchdowns. He had 1,005 yards receiving and 4 touchdowns. He joined Roger Craig and Marshall Faulk as the only running backs in NFL history with 1,000 yards rushing and receiving in the same season.

He ended the year with 2,392 yards from scrimmage, third most in NFL history. His 116 catches were the most in NFL history by a running back, and while touching the ball 403 times, he did not lose a single fumble all season.

"You always have to look for something to look on and build as a positive, and that's certainly one of them," linebacker Luke Kuechly said of McCaffrey's season. "Not a lot of people are able to do what he does. Not a lot of people are able to play the amount of snaps he does at that position. He's a special player. I know the season didn't go obviously the way we wanted it to. You can still take away from the fact that Christian had a special year, and special years like that always deserve to be recognized."[xxxiii]

McCaffrey was named to the Pro Bowl and first team All-Pro for the first time in his career. He finished third in Offensive MVP voting.

But at the end of the season, McCaffrey said that he felt great after having more than 400 touches. That would come back to haunt him.

Injuries

The 2020 season was going to be one of many changes for the Carolina Panthers, and it began at the top. To replace longtime head coach Ron Rivera, who was let go near the end of the 2019 season, the Panthers hired Baylor coach Matt Ruhle.

In the offseason, the team parted ways with former MVP Cam Newton and brought Teddy Bridgewater on board as their new starting quarterback. They also said goodbye to longtime linebacker Luke Kuechly, who decided to retire after spending his entire eight-year NFL career with the Panthers.

The Panthers also made a long-term commitment to McCaffrey. They signed the back to a four-year, $64-million extension, making him the highest-paid running back in NFL history.

"I don't know where to start saying thank you," McCaffrey said. "First off, just to the whole Panthers organization for believing in me and allowing me to continue my career in the play where it started. Thank you to Mr. Tepper for believing in me and thank you to Marty Hurney for believing in me, Coach Rhule for believing in me. I couldn't be more excited. We have a great thing going, a fresh start, and I'm more than excited. So, to all the Panthers fans out there, I hope you're as excited as I am. We're going to go out there and win some games and give you everything we've got."xxxiv

In Week 1's loss to the Los Vegas Raiders, McCaffrey did not disappoint. He rushed for 97 yards and 2 touchdowns, but his efforts were again wasted by the Panthers.

Against Tampa and their new quarterback, Tom Brady, McCaffrey scored a touchdown early in the fourth quarter but never returned to the game. Two plays earlier, he had rolled his ankle but managed to stay in the game.

"I hate it for him. No one wants to be out there and play more than Christian does, but everything happens for a reason," Rhule said. "I'm sure he'll rehab. I'm sure he's rehabbing right now. I talked to him earlier today and he'll get back as soon as he can."xxxv

McCaffrey would miss the next six weeks of the season with a high ankle sprain. In his absence, the Panthers went 3-3.

He returned just in time for a Week 9 matchup against the Kansas City Chiefs. McCaffrey scored 2 touchdowns and had 151 yards from scrimmage in his return, but late in the game, he suffered a shoulder injury. He ended up spraining the AC Joint in his shoulder. That injury would cost him another four games.

McCaffrey made it back for a Week 14 game, but during warmups, he injured his thigh. This time, he was diagnosed with a thigh strain. He was put on injured reserve and missed the rest of the season.

In all, McCaffrey played in just three games in the 2020 season, scoring six touchdowns. It was déjà vu in Carolina as the team matched their losing record of the previous season, finishing 5-11 and missing the postseason once again. But they were optimistic about the 2021 season ahead.

With McCaffrey back, the Panthers started the 2021 season 3-0. But in the team's Week 3 win over Houston, he suffered a hamstring strain that would cost him five games.

"We'll be all right without him," New Panthers quarterback Sam Darnold said. "Obviously, we want him back, but I want him to take his time right now and make sure he's good for the end of the season."[xxxvi]

Without him, the Panthers lost four of five games. McCaffrey returned against New England, but the Panthers could not win the game. After a win over Atlanta and a loss to Washington, the Panthers traveled to Miami. Early in the game, McCaffrey left the field with an apparent ankle injury.

A few days later, the Panthers announced that McCaffrey would miss the rest of the season with another high ankle sprain. When he played in 2021, the

Panthers were 4-3. Without McCaffrey, they were 1-9, including losing the last five games of the season.

Back to the Bay

After two lost seasons plagued by injuries, Christian McCaffrey was ready to get back to work with the Carolina Panthers.

"I feel great, feel the best I've ever felt," McCaffrey said. "I'm ready to go. I know my teammates are as well, and we're all excited to be here."[xxxvii]

But Coach Matt Rhule had to be careful with McCaffrey. The team still lacked a clear starting quarterback heading into the 2022 season (a position that had lately become a veritable revolving door for them), and McCaffrey was going to be his only weapon on offense.

"We're going to do maybe a couple things different in training camp, but I think our training camps with Christian have been right," Rhule said. "I think he's entered the season and been really healthy and productive early. But he is a year older. As players get older, they get a little bit more break-in time and all those things. So we might give him some time here and there."[xxxvii]

In the first two weeks of the season, Carolina lost both games by a combined five points. McCaffrey only had one touchdown but did rush for 100 yards in a Week 2 loss to the Giants.

After beating the reeling Saints, the Panthers lost three-straight games and were not competitive in any of them. McCaffrey did not break 100 yards in any of those games and he only scored 2 touchdowns.

At that point in the season, the Panthers were 1-5 and looking lifeless. That was when the rumors started. The Carolina Panthers were considering trading McCaffrey to get more draft capital.

Prior to Week 7, the Panthers pulled the trigger, trading McCaffrey to the San Francisco 49ers.

McCaffrey was headed back to the Bay Area, where he had played his college ball at Stanford. In return, the Panthers received the 49ers' second, third, and fourth-round draft picks in 2023 and a fifth-round pick in 2024.

"In hindsight, I firmly believe it's the best thing that ever happened to me," McCaffrey said after the season. "I say this with the utmost respect. This is a family. It's the first time I felt like, even alumni, just getting to know these guys, it's special, it's different, and there's a reason it's sustainable and has been for so long. The word I would use now is, just very proud to be a part of this organization."[xxxviii]

But while the trade turned out great for McCaffrey, his initial reaction was anger. The Panthers had told him that they were not planning on trading him when the rumors first started, but then they got the 49ers' offer and made the trade.

"Obviously, I took it personally," McCaffrey said. "When you get traded, it's one team saying, 'We don't value you as much anymore and so we're going to get rid of you.' That's how I took it and that's what it is but I know it's a business. Just another chip on my shoulder and here I am."[xxxix]

McCaffrey went from worst to first. In his first week with the 49ers, he played sparingly as he was learning the playbook. The following week, the 49ers took on the Rams, who had also been trying to acquire McCaffrey but failed.

In the game, Christian McCaffrey became the 11th player in NFL history to run, throw, and catch a touchdown pass in a blowout win over Los Angeles.

"Both of my little brothers are quarterbacks, so I learned a lot from them," McCaffrey said with a smile. "I used to always want to play quarterback just because it was the best position. It helps when someone is wide open as well. I think the biggest thing is coming out with a win, and playing the second half like that, too. I think the thing I'm most happy about is just this whole team welcoming me in with open arms."[xl]

McCaffrey now had a creative play caller in 49ers head coach Kyle Shanahan. And best of all, Shanahan and McCaffrey had known each other since McCaffrey was two years old. Kyle's father, Mike, was the head coach for the Denver Broncos when McCaffrey's father, Ed, was winning Super Bowls for the team.

With their new offensive weapon and a solid defense, the 49ers started rolling. After the win over the Rams, San Francisco went on to win nine games in a row. For the first time since his rookie season, McCaffrey was headed to the playoffs. The 49ers won the NFC West and were the second seed in the NFC behind the Philadelphia Eagles.

In the opening round, the 49ers took on division rival Seattle, but even though San Francisco had practically sailed into the postseason, they also suffered their share of injuries. Most notably, they were down to playing the game with their third-string quarterback, Brock Purdy.

McCaffrey helped lighten the load with 119 yards rushing and a touchdown catch. But the Seahawks were still up by a point at the half. Then, in the second half, the 49ers bombed the Seahawks. San Fran scored 25 straight points to win the game and head into the Divisional Round against Dallas. For McCaffrey, it was his first career playoff win.

The Cowboys and the 49ers traded field goals throughout the first three quarters. Finally, in the fourth quarter, McCaffrey put San Fran up by seven with a rushing touchdown that was set up by an amazing catch by tight end George Kittle. That was their only touchdown scored in the game, but the 49ers held on to win 19-12.

For the first time in his career, Christian McCaffrey was headed to the NFC Championship game. The 49ers would face the top-seeded Philadelphia Eagles in Philly.

It was a disaster right from the start. Starting quarterback Brock Purdy suffered a UCL injury on the game's first series and should not have returned. He literally could not lift his arm to throw a football. The score was briefly tied 7-7 on a McCaffrey touchdown run in the second quarter but after that, it was all Philadelphia. By the third quarter, San Fran was down to their fourth-string quarterback, Josh Johnson, and he suffered a concussion. So, Purdy was sent back into the game to hand the ball off but could do little more than that. In the end, the Eagles won the game 31-7 and were on their way to the Super Bowl.

"It's really tough," McCaffrey said. "You don't want to make excuses obviously. It just sucks because we wish we had a healthy quarterback for a full game. It's a really good team that we played. But it feels like something got stolen from you."[xli]

In a season that saw McCaffrey go from one of the worst teams in the league to one of the best, he rushed for 1,139 yards and 8 touchdowns. He added 741 receiving yards and 5 touchdowns. In three playoff games, he rushed for 238 yards and 2 touchdowns. He caught 61 yards and another touchdown. He was named to the Pro Bowl for the third time in his career and came in second to Geno Smith for Comeback Player of the Year.

Chapter 4: Personal Life

How many times has someone been scrolling through social media and liked a photo of a complete stranger? Nothing usually comes of it. But most people are not Christian McCaffrey.

In May 2019, Christian liked a photo of former Miss Universe Olivia Culpo. Two months later, they were introduced through mutual friends. At first, Olivia was not interested in dating an athlete, but she went on the date anyway.

Eventually, she started showing up for Carolina Panthers home games wearing his jersey. Olivia has been on the cover of *Vogue* and the *Sports Illustrated* Swimsuit Edition as a model, but donning that Panthers jersey was her most telling outfit of all. The couple started taking vacations together and even got a puppy.

"He's just the best, I feel like he is really everything that I could ever ask for," Olivia said. "So, I never have to worry about anything. I think that was the reason why I didn't want to date an athlete, no offense, because there is a reputation there. He just comes from a great family. We have a lot in common in that respect. I feel like you can really tell who a person is by the people that raise them, and I just love his parents so much. They have a great relationship."[xlii]

In April 2023, after four years together, Christian proposed and Olivia accepted. No date has been set for the wedding yet, but rumor has it that Olivia has begun planning the event. Their puppy, now a strapping golden doodle named Oliver, is now in training to be their ring bearer.

Speaking of training, in the offseason, Christian still returns home to Colorado to work out at his old high school, but also to spend quality time with his family. It allows him to be close with his mom, dad, and also his brothers. Ed is now the head football coach at

Northern Colorado University, so it is hard for the two of them to get together during the football season.

Christian is now legendary for his training and fitness regimens but confesses that Doritos and Oreos are his Kryptonite, something that fans have caught onto over the years as well. He even traded a pair of autographed cleats to 13-year-old fan Mason Sims for some Cool Ranch Doritos and a bag of Oreos during camp in 2022.

Christian has a few other talents as well. He loves music and can play the piano and harmonica very well. You can see videos of him playing on his Instagram, including an impressive cover of Billy Joel's "Piano Man." He also loves movies and television, and minored in film in college. He even has a production credit to his name, the 2022 film *Unicorn Town*, about an underdog football team in a small German town.

Christian has also parlayed his own successes into giving back. It is clear that he is a class act, both professionally and personally, and is perpetually focused on giving back to his community and helping those who are less fortunate. He started the Christian McCaffrey Foundation to raise money to support military families and veterans. The Foundation's main fundraiser is a yearly online Madden Tournament.

Christian's friends from around the NFL take each other on in a game of Madden as their team. Last year, the tournament brought together the likes of Saquon Barkley, Dalvin Cook, Solomon Thomas, and Austin Ekeler. The winner was Fred Warner of the 49ers.

In 2020, the Foundation put together the "22 and You" drive, which raised money to support frontline workers in North and South Carolina during the COVID-19 Pandemic. Christian also wanted kids to be able to join in with his Madden Tournament, so he has donated hundreds of gaming systems to children's hospitals in North Carolina, Colorado, and California.

Chapter 5: Legacy

Christian McCaffrey's legacy is secured in the NFL. He is one of only three players in league history with 1,000 yards rushing and receiving in a season. He also has three seasons with at least 1,000 yards rushing and 700 yards receiving.

McCaffrey's legacy will not come from climbing the NFL's all-time leaders in rushing. Instead, his legacy will come from his all-purpose yards. He is currently not in the top 250 NFL players all-time in all-purpose yards, but he has only played six seasons in the NFL. And in two of those seasons, he only played 10 games due to injury.

McCaffrey said it himself that the trade to San Francisco may be the best thing that ever happened to him. In just half a season with the 49ers, he played in more playoff games than he did in his first five seasons with Carolina.

Furthermore, working with the offensive genius of Kyle Shanahan will only help to get the most out of McCaffrey. It also helps that the 49ers have a much better offense with more weapons than McCaffrey ever had in Carolina.

His legacy in college will also one day get him into the College Football Hall of Fame. His sophomore season was one of the greatest seasons in FBS history. If it had not been for an unworldly season by Derrick Henry, McCaffrey would have certainly won the Heisman Trophy.

McCaffrey is still only 27 years old. He has two years remaining on his contract with the 49ers. Even after that, he's still only 29, with plenty of good years left to play. It is easy to surmise that his best is yet to come.

Not bad for the McCaffrey's smallest child. It's all in the bloodlines!

Final Word/About the Author

Wow! You made it to the end of this book, and you're reading the About the Author section? Now that's impressive and puts you in the top 1% of readers.

Since you're curious about me, I was born and raised in Norwalk, Connecticut. Growing up, I could often be found spending many nights watching basketball, soccer, and football matches with my father in the family living room. I love sports and everything that sports can embody. I believe that sports are one of the most genuine forms of competition, heart, and determination. I write my works to learn more about influential athletes in the hopes that from my writing, you the reader can walk away inspired to put in an equal if not greater amount of hard work and perseverance to pursue your goals.

I've written these stories for over a decade, and loved every moment of it. When I look back on my life, I am most proud of not just having covered so many different athletes' inspirational stories, but for all the times I got e-mails or handwritten letters from readers on the impact my books have had on them.

So thank you from the bottom of my heart for allowing me to do work I find meaningful. I am incredibly grateful for you and your support.

If you're new to my sports biography books, welcome. I have goodies for you as a thank you from me in the pages ahead.

Before we get there though, I have a question for you…

Were you inspired at any point in this book?
If so, would you help someone else get inspired too?

You see, my mission is to inspire sports fans of all ages around the world that anything is possible through hard work and perseverance…but the only way to accomplish this mission is by reaching everyone.

So here's my ask from you:

Most people, regardless of what the saying tells them to do, judge a book by its cover (and its reviews).

If you enjoyed *Christian McCaffrey: The Inspiring Story of One of Football's Star Running Backs,* please help inspire another person needing to hear this story by leaving a review.

Doing so takes less than a minute, and that dose of inspiration can change another person's life in more ways than you can even imagine.

To get that generous 'feel good' feeling and help another person, all you have to do is take 60 seconds and leave a review.

☆☆☆☆☆ ✍

If you're on Audible: hit the three dots in the top right of your device, click rate & review, then leave a few sentences about the book with a star rating.

<u>If you're reading on Kindle or an e-reader</u>: scroll to the bottom of the book, then swipe up and it will prompt a review for you.

<u>If for some reason these have changed</u>: you can head back to Amazon and leave a review right on the book's page.

Thank you for helping another person, and for your support of my writing as an independent author.

Clayton

Like what you read? Then you'll love these too!

This book is one of hundreds of stories I've written. If you enjoyed this story on Christian McCaffrey, you'll love my other sports biography book series too.

You can find them by visiting my website at claytongeoffreys.com or by scanning the QR code below to follow my author page on Amazon.

Here's a little teaser about each of my sports biography book series:

Football Biography Books: This series covers the stories of over 50 NFL greats such as Peyton Manning, Tom Brady, and Patrick Mahomes, and more.

Basketball Biography Books: This series covers the stories of over 100 NBA greats such as Stephen Curry, LeBron James, Michael Jordan, and more.

Basketball Leadership Biography Books: This series covers the stories of basketball coaching greats such as Steve Kerr, Gregg Popovich, John Wooden, and more.

Baseball Biography Books: This series covers the stories of over 40 MLB greats such as Aaron Judge, Shohei Ohtani, Mike Trout, and more.

Soccer Biography Books: This series covers the stories of tennis greats such as Neymar, Harry Kane, Robert Lewandowski, and more.

Tennis Biography Books: This series covers the stories of tennis greats such as Serena Williams, Rafael Nadal, Andy Roddick, and more.

Women's Basketball Biography Books: This series covers the stories of many WNBA greats such as Diana Taurasi, Sue Bird, Sabrina Ionescu, and more.

Lastly, if you'd like to join my exclusive list where I let you know about my latest books, and gift you free copies of some of my other books, go to **claytongeoffreys.com/goodies**.

Or, if you don't like typing, scan the following QR code here to go there directly. See you there!

Clayton

References

[i] Saunders, Patrick. "Broncos' Ed McCaffrey, Wife, Lisa, Both Come From Long Line of Athletes." The Denver Post. Nov. 4, 2015.

[ii] Ballard, Chris. "Mr. Everything: Christian McCaffrey is the Nation's Best Player, but He Can't be Summed Up by His Achievements." Sports Illustrated. May 17, 2018.

[iii] Castillo, Jarrod. "CMC's Mom, Lisa, Shares Hilarious Gender Reveal Story." NBC Sports.Com. Feb. 9, 2023. Web.

[iv] Barrows, Matt. "Where Does Christian McCaffrey Get His Speed?" The Athletic. Jan. 13, 2023.

[v] Casey, Ryan. "Running Back Christian McCaffrey is Valor Christian's Offensive Weapon." The Denver Post. July 9, 2011.

[vi] Devlin, Neil. "Christian McCaffrey Makes Run Into Record Books." The Denver Post. Nov. 9, 2013.

[vii] "Stanford Routs Aggies." Go Stanford.Com. August 30, 2014 Web.

[viii] "Cardinal Falls to No. 25 Utah." Go Stanford.Com. Nov. 15, 2014. Web.

[ix] "Foster Farms Bowl Blowout." Go Stanford.Com Dec. 30, 2014. Web.

[x] "Defensive Domination." Go Stanford.Com. Sept. 12, 2015. Web.

[xi] "Cardinal Take Los Angeles." Go Stanford.Com. Sept. 19, 2015. Web.

[xii] "McCaffrey Runs Wild." Go Stanford.Com. Sept. 26, 2015. Web.

[xiii] "Statement Made." Go Stanford.Com. Oct. 16, 2015. Web.

[xiv] "Six Straight." Go Stanford.Com. Oct. 24, 2015. Web.

[xv] "McCaffrey Outruns Ralph." Go Stanford.Com. Nov. 7, 2015. Web.

[xvi] "Pac 12 Champions." Go Stanford.Com. Dec. 5, 2015. Web.

[xvii] Hart, Torrey. "Christian McCaffrey Was Told He Lost a Heisman Vote Because the Voter Didn't Stay Up for His Games." Yahoo! Sports.Com. Nov. 21, 2019. Web.

[xviii] Newton, David. "Heisman Hijacked? Christian McCaffrey Miffed But Not at Derrick Henry." ESPN.Com. Nov. 1, 2019. Web.

[xix] Ballad, Chris. "Mr. Everything: Christian McCaffrey is the Nation's Best Player, but he can't be Summed up by His Achievements." Sports Illustrated. May 17, 2016.

[xx] "Huskies Take Down Cardinal." Go Stanford.Com. Sept. 30, 2016. Web.

[xxi] "Home Setback." Go Stanford.Com. Oct. 8, 2016. Web.

[xxii] "The Axe Stays Home." Go Stanford.Com. Nov. 19, 2016. Web.

[xxiii] "Christian McCaffrey Won't Play in Sun Bowl." ESPN.Com. Dec. 19, 2016. Web.

[xxiv] Burke, Chris. "2017 NFL Draft Countdown: No. 13 Christian McCaffrey." Sports Illustrated. April 4, 2017.

[xxv] Wilson, Ryan. "NFL GMs Asking Christian McCaffrey Why He Skipped Stanford's Bowl Game." CBS Sports.Com. March 3, 2017. Web.

[xxvi] Reed, Steve. "McCaffrey's Shiftiness Turning Heads at Panther's Camp." Daily Commercial. Aug. 2, 2017.

[xxvii] "Looking Back at Christian McCaffrey's Rookie Season." Panthers.Com. Jan. 10, 2018 Web.

[xxviii] "Newton's 4 TDS Lift Panthers Over Bengals." CBS Sports.Com Sept. 23, 2018. Web.

[xxix] Henson, Max. "Christian McCaffrey Reacts To Pro Bowl Omission." Panthers.Com Dec. 18, 2018. Web.

[xxx] Hall, Brandon. "Why Christian McCaffrey is Training Like a Track Athlete this Offseason." Stack.Com. April 19, 2019. Web.

[xxxi] Shook, Nick. "Carolina Panthers Fire Head Coach Ron Rivera." NFL.Com. Dec. 3, 2019. Web.

[xxxii] "McCaffrey's Season Not All for Naught." USA Today. Dec. 15, 2019.

[xxxiii] Voth, Bill. "Christian McCaffrey's Remarkable Year During Panthers' Disappointing Season Proves 'It Takes a Village.'" Panthers.Com. Dec. 29, 2019. Web.

[xxxiv] Simmons, Myles. "Panthers Sign Christian McCaffrey to Contract Extension Through 2025." Panthers.Com. April 16, 2020. Web.

[xxxv] Simmons, Myles. "Christian McCaffrey to Miss Multiple Weeks with High Ankle Sprain." Panthers.Com. Sept. 21, 2020. Web.

[xxxvi] Grant, Gordon. "Panthers RB Christian McCaffrey Strained Hamstring Vs. Texans." NFL.Com. Sept. 23, 2021. Web.

[xxxvii] Stone, Augusta. "Christian McCaffrey Ready to Roll." Panthers.Com. July 26, 2022. Web.

[xxxviii] Patra, Kevin. "RB Christian McCaffrey: Trade to 49ers Was the 'Best Thing That Ever Happened to Me." NFL.Com. May 17, 2023. Web.

[xxxix] Wagoner, Nick. "Christian McCaffrey Trade from Panthers to 49ers: Inside Story." ESPN.Com. Jan 27, 2023. Web.

[xl] "McCaffrey Throws, Catches, Rushes for TDs, Niners Rout Rams." ESPN.Com. Oct. 30, 2022. Web.

[xli] Bumbaca, Chris. "Christian McCaffrey Says NFC Championship Game was 'Stolen' from San Francisco 49ers." USA Today. Feb. 9, 2023.

[xlii] Kaloi, Stephanie. "Olivia Culpo and Christian McCaffrey Relationship Timeline." People Magazine. May 11, 2023.

Printed in Great Britain
by Amazon